COLLINS

SKYWATCH

Written by
Rhoda Nottridge

Illustrated by
Arcana Artists and Bob Reed

Note to parents and teachers

This beautifully illustrated book is an ideal introduction to astronomy for children from 8 to 11. At the end of the book there is a glossary of new words and an index which will help children come to consider books as works of reference.

WARNING: Never look directly at the sun.

CONTENTS

INTRODUCTION

For thousands of years, men and women have looked into the night sky and marvelled at the beauty of the stars and planets.

To the Greeks and Romans, these stars and planets had been put in the sky by their gods and goddesses. Legends arose about heroes such as Orion the Hunter and Auriga the Charioteer who were placed in the sky as starry constellations as a reward for their exploits on Earth.

In the second century BC, the Greek scientist Hipparchus charted the position of more than 1,000 stars and was the first person to make a scientific analysis of the movement of heavenly bodies and the Earth's seasons.

Sailors had used the stars to guide them long before the early Middle Ages when the Arabs refined the astrolabe, an instrument used by Hipparchus in his observations of the stars, and it became an invaluable navigation aid.

Our knowledge of the stars and planets broadened in the sixteenth and seventeenth centuries. In 1543, Nicolaus Copernicus put forward his theory that the Earth orbited the Sun.

In 1576, Tycho Brahe, a Danish astronomer, made instruments with which he mapped the movements of the planets with great accuracy.

In 1609, Johannes Kepler used Copernicus's and Brahe's findings to prove that all the planets moved around the Sun. In the same year, Galileo built his first telescope through which he observed the Moon, Venus and Jupiter. It was not long before astronomers all over the world were making bigger and better telescopes. In 1668, Sir Isaac Newton made an improved telescope that used a mirror rather than a lens to collect light.

Since then, telescopes have become much more efficient, and today, with radio telescopes, manned space flights and space probes deep into space, our knowledge of the Solar System and Milky Way galaxy, and of the galaxies that lie beyond ours, has increased hugely.

This book tells you about planets, stars and other things such as comets to be seen in the sky. It also contains eight star maps that show you some of what can be seen in the night sky looking north and south during the four seasons of the year.

What is a star?

You may often have looked up at the beautiful lights that twinkle in the night sky. You know they are called stars and you may know the names of some of them, but what exactly are they?

Although they look so small and fragile suspended in the sky, stars are huge, fiercely hot balls of gases. Stars are born in the great clouds of gas and dust that exist in space. A star starts to form when gas and dust collect together into a thicker and thicker mass under the pull of **gravity**.*

YELLOW DWARF

The mass shrinks and becomes ball-shaped. As it shrinks, it starts to heat up. It becomes hotter and hotter until it starts to glow and shine as a new star. The temperature at its centre would now be about 16,000,000 degrees Celsius ($^{\circ}$C). A tiny piece of coal that hot would kill you if you were standing 200 kilometres away from it. It is this extreme heat that makes stars glow in the sky.

The Sun is the nearest star to Earth. You may wonder why other stars look so tiny in the sky compared to the Sun. It is because they are millions

RED GIANT

upon millions of kilometres away. The next nearest star to Earth is called Proxima Centauri. If you were travelling in a car at 90 km/h, it would take you 30 million years to reach it.

Stars vary in heat, size and colour. They can be blue, white, yellow or red. They all live for millions of years, but as they get older they change and eventually die.

A star about the size of our Sun is called a yellow dwarf. It has a surface temperature of about 5,500°C. As a yellow dwarf, it will shine for about 10,000 million years. When the gases in its centre are nearly burnt out, it begins to die. The star then swells up in size, until it is perhaps a hundred times its size as a yellow dwarf. As it expands, it cools down and becomes red, so it is called a red giant. When the Sun turns into a red giant, which will not be for at least 5,000 million years, it will swell up to such a size that it will engulf the planet Mercury and maybe Venus, and scorch the Earth.

The meaning of words in bold is explained in the glossary at the back of the book.

Red giants eventually collapse and become tiny white stars called white dwarfs, which continue to cool down.
   They are only small in comparison to red giants and may still be the size of Earth. No one knows exactly what happens to white dwarfs when they have cooled down completely. Probably they become small, dark lumps floating through space, which are called black dwarfs.

WHITE DWARF

Astronomers reckon that there could be as many as 1,500 billion billion stars in the **universe**. Some are up to 1,000 times larger than the Sun. When such a massive star dies, it is a spectacular sight. Its centre becomes so hot that it explodes and blasts itself apart as a supernova, brighter than millions of suns. On average, one supernova occurs somewhere in the universe every second.

SUPERNOVA

NEUTRON STAR

The material left at the centre after a
supernova becomes a tiny **neutron
star**, which may measure only about
20 kilometres across. However, the
material making up the neutron star is
so dense that a teaspoonful of it would
weigh about 1,000 million tonnes.
Some very large stars create an
enormous pull of gravity inwards
when they collapse and do not even
leave a neutron star. The pull
becomes so strong that anything
nearby is pulled inwards; not even
light can escape. The region of space
where this enormous gravitational
pull acts is known as a black hole.

7

Star Clusters and Nebulae

Have you ever noticed fuzzy patches amongst the stars, that look a little like clouds? The vast expanse of space between the stars is not completely empty, but contains here and there particles of gas and dust. In places the particles gather together in denser clouds we call nebulae (singular, nebula). We see some nebulae when they reflect the light of nearby stars. We see others when they absorb the radiation from young stars within them, and this lights them up. Dark nebulae blot out the stars behind them completely.

ORION NEBULA

CRAB NEBULA

Nebulae can be seen in many of the constellations. A constellation is a group of stars, whose bright stars appear to make a recognizable pattern. Each constellation is named after this pattern. In the constellation called Orion, there is the famous Orion Nebula, which you can see without a **telescope**.

The Crab Nebula, in the constellation Taurus, the Bull, is thought to be the remains of a massive supernova which Chinese astronomers saw exploding in 1054. This cloud of dust and gas is the visible remains of the supernova.

Not all bright patches in the night sky are nebulae. Some are groups of stars, very close together, which are called star clusters. These clusters come in two kinds.

Open clusters are made up of a loose group of hundreds or thousands of young stars, which are moving through space together. They are not arranged in any particular way and astronomers think of them as young because they are less than 100 million years old!

The best known open cluster, which you can easily see, is called the Pleiades, or the Seven Sisters. At first sight, it appears to be just a misty patch of light, but on close examination you can make out five, or with very good eyesight, even more of the stars. The Seven Sisters can be found in the constellation Taurus.

PLEIADES

GLOBULAR CLUSTER

The second type of star cluster is called a globular cluster. This is a cluster of tens of thousands of stars, packed tightly in a sphere-shape. The stars tend to be much older than those in open clusters. Towards the centre of the cluster they are packed very closely together by the force of gravity. This is why they have stayed together for millions of years. A globular cluster can be seen in the constellation of Hercules.

If the Earth were in the middle of a globular cluster, the light from the closely packed stars would be so bright that it would be like having a full moon shimmering every night.

There are nearly 200 globular clusters and 1,000 open clusters in our **galaxy** alone. This galaxy is called the Milky Way.

The Milky Way and other Galaxies

Astronomers think that less than two parts in every one hundred thousand parts of space contains galaxies and the rest is dark and empty, a void. However, there are billions of galaxies in the universe, and our **Solar System** is just a small part of a huge collection of stars which make up just one galaxy, called the Milky Way.

Galaxies are huge systems of stars. Most galaxies are spiral- or egg-shaped. Spiral galaxies look like a spinning Catherine wheel firework. Everything in the Milky Way is moving slowly round the centre of the spiral. Stars close to the middle take about ten million Earth-years to move right round the spiral, while the Sun, which is farther out, takes about 225 million Earth-years to go round. The Sun has travelled less than half-way round the galaxy since the days when dinosaurs roamed the Earth.

The Milky Way is part of what is called the Local Group, which is a collection of about 30 galaxies.

The largest galaxy in this group is the spiral Andromeda galaxy, which is just visible to the naked eye. The Milky Way is the second largest galaxy, followed by the Triangulum galaxy.

There are many other groups of galaxies. The Virgo group includes over 1,000 galaxies. Altogether, there are 15,000 million galaxies in the universe. All the galaxies are moving away from each other at continually increasing speed, further and further out into the darkness of space.

ANDROMEDA GALAXY

Quasars

The brightest, most remote objects from Earth are also the most mysterious. A quasi-stellar radio source, called a quasar for short, was first discovered in 1963. A scientist researching radio signals from the heavens found that they were coming from an object that was not, as he first thought, a star. Since then hundreds of quasars have been discovered, some so far away that their light has taken over 13,000 million years to reach us.

In general, a quasar seems to be very much smaller than a galaxy, yet is brighter than hundreds of galaxies put together! Astronomers are not certain what quasars are and why they shine so brightly. But many people believe that they are the very bright centres of far-distant galaxies, and think that they get their enormous energy from a massive black hole at their centre. Huge black holes are also thought to be the energy source behind radio galaxies, bodies that give off millions of times more energy than ordinary galaxies, mainly in the form of radio waves rather than light.

Quasars and radio galaxies are examples of what are called active galaxies, which have black holes at their centre. They could be different views of the matter that swirls around black holes.

QUASAR

The Solar System

The Solar System is the name we give to the Sun and the family of bodies that **orbit** it in space. This includes nine planets, one being the Earth. The Sun is about 4,600,000,000 years old. Its diameter is about 1,392,500 kilometres, and its mass is nearly 750 times greater than all of the planets put together. If you think of the Earth as being the size of a ping-pong ball, the Sun will be the size of a beach-ball.

The Sun is extremely hot. It has a surface temperature of about 5,500°C. It burns up some 4 million tonnes of **hydrogen** every second to produce the energy to keep shining. Its rays take 8 minutes and 20 seconds to reach us. The Earth receives only a tiny fraction of the energy the Sun puts out.

Earth is the third closest planet to

MERCURY

THE SUN

the Sun. Mercury is closest of all. It is hard to see because it remains so close to the Sun. Occasionally it can be seen as a bright, pinkish star in the west after sunset or in the east before dawn. During the day, the temperature on Mercury averages 350°C, which is seven times hotter than the highest temperature ever recorded on Earth. No life form known to humans can survive in such heat. At night, the temperature drops to an unbelievably cold −170° C.

Mercury is named after the swift-footed messenger of the gods in Roman

VENUS

MARS

EARTH

mythology, because it travels faster around the Sun (172,248 km/h) than any other planet. It takes 88 days to complete one orbit, compared with Earth's 365.25 days (one year). Pluto, usually the furthest planet, takes no less than 248 years for each orbit.

Venus is the brightest planet visible to the naked eye, and is sometimes visible in daylight. It is brilliant white and appears brighter than Sirius.

In some months Venus shines in the west at sunset, when it is called the Evening Star. In other months it shines in the East at sunrise, when it is called the Morning Star. Temperatures on Venus soar to nearly 500°C, making the planet far too hot to permit life forms as we know them.

Mars is the next planet in the Solar System going out from Earth. It is often called the Red Planet because of its reddish-orange colour. In appearance Mars is easy to confuse with a real star. Like Earth, Mars has frozen polar caps and it also has a canyon, called Mariner Valley, that is long enough to stretch from one side of the United States to the other.

After Mars, going away from the Sun, come the planets Jupiter, Saturn, Uranus, Neptune and Pluto. They are all too cold to support life forms. Jupiter is the largest of all the planets, with a diameter of 142,800 kilometres. Like the three other giant planets, it is made up of a rocky core, surrounded by a vast ocean of liquid gas. Jupiter appears in the sky as a brilliant yellow star, and can be seen for several months of the year as it follows its slow path around the Sun. The four largest of its many moons can be seen quite easily with binoculars. On Jupiter, the force of gravity is about 2.5 times greater than it is on Earth.

SATURN

JUPITER

Saturn is the second biggest planet and is perhaps the most beautiful because it is surrounded by particles of dust and ice that look like rings. Saturn has strong hurricane winds blowing round its **equator** at speeds of 1,770 km/h.

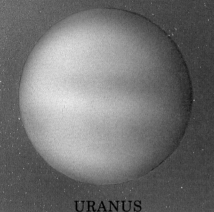

URANUS

PLUTO

NEPTUNE

Uranus and Neptune are cold balls of gas and liquid gas which are similar in size, but not in appearance. Whereas Uranus is a featureless blue-green colour, Neptune is deep blue, with flecks of white cloud. One year on Uranus lasts 84 Earth-years; on Neptune, 164.8 Earth-years. The most recently discovered planet in the Solar System, in 1930, was Pluto.

It lies on average 5,900,000,000 kilometres from the Earth and would take about 400 years to fly to in an aeroplane. Some scientists think that there may even be another planet beyond it. Every year space **probes** journey deeper and deeper into unknown space and send back information that constantly changes our knowledge of the Solar System.

Comets

A comet is one of the most dramatic sights in the sky at night. When you see one, it looks like a huge snowball hurtling across the sky. Comets are made up of ice and dust, which probably clumped together into a ball during the formation of the Solar System.

Comets travel through space for the most part unseen. They become visible from Earth only when they approach the Sun. The heat from the Sun gradually causes the ice in a comet's core to melt and **evaporate** into gas and so releases the dust. A cloud of gas and dust is produced, which starts to glow as it reflects sunlight.

Comets travel at incredible speeds. When they are close to the Sun they can reach speeds of up to 2,000,000 km/h. When a comet is travelling slowly it is still moving at around 1,000 km/h.

Comets often grow a kind of tail. It is made up of gas and dust, pushed away from the core by a stream of particles from the Sun. Often a comet develops two distinct tails. One is made up of glowing gas, the other of shining dust.

Sometimes a tail trails behind a comet for vast distances. In 1843 a comet named the Great Comet was seen. Astronomers were able to calculate that its tail was 330,000,000 kilometres long.

The orbits of many comets are unknown but others travel past the Sun regularly, such as Encke's comet, which can be seen from Earth every 3.3 years. Astronomers record the movements of comets to predict when they will return. A comet named after an astronomer called Delavan was first seen in 1914. It is not expected to be seen again from our planet for more than 24 million years.

Comets are often named after the astronomers who first spot them. Back in 240 BC, a comet was recorded and it has since reappeared on many occasions. It was seen in 1066 and is pictured in the famous Bayeux Tapestry, which also depicts William the Conqueror and the Battle of Hastings. In 1682, an English astronomer called Edmund Halley saw this comet and correctly calculated that it would return every 76 years. His prediction was correct and it returned in 1758.

ABOVE: In this section of the Bayeux Tapestry, we can see Halley's Comet zooming through the sky. RIGHT: The overlay display on this picture of the Giotto Control Room, shows the time to Giotto's closest approach and the distance from the centre of the comet.

This century, Halley's Comet, as it became known, was seen in 1910 and again in 1986. The European space probe Giotto travelled very close to the centre of the comet in 1986. It sent back information which showed that the comet's core was about 15 kilometres long and, surprisingly, looked like black velvet close up. Halley's Comet will next appear in the sky in 2062. How old will you be when it returns?

Asteroids

In the last two hundred years, astronomers have discovered a belt of small planets between Mars and Jupiter. These planets are called asteroids. They are around 420,000,000 kilometres from the Sun and orbit around it, just like the other planets in our Solar System.

Occasionally, asteroids may stray too close to a large planet and be drawn in by the planet's gravity. They become **satellites** of the planet. It is quite likely that the two small satellites of Mars are asteroids captured this way.

CERES

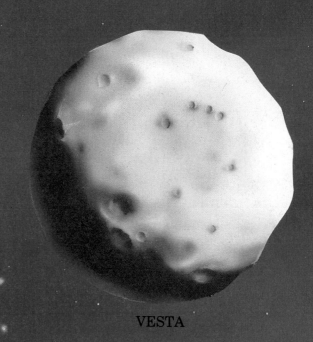

VESTA

HECTOR

Astronomers estimate that there are at least 100,000 asteroids. They range in size from a few hundred metres across to about 1,000 kilometres across, which is the size of the largest asteroid, Ceres. Asteroids come in a variety of shapes. Some look like bricks and one, called Hector, looks like a dumbbell.

All asteroids are rocky. They shine by reflecting sunlight. The only asteroid visible to the naked eye is called Vesta. It has a diameter of about 520 kilometres and was discovered in 1807.

Eclipses

In 213 BC, Chinese people were terrified by something they saw in the sky. It appeared as though a bite had been taken out of the Sun. Then more and more of the Sun disappeared until the sky was dark. There was nothing but a thin circle of light around the area where the Sun had been. A terrible dragon had eaten the Sun!

The Chinese beat drums and screamed up at the monster and to their relief it slowly spat the Sun out again.

What the Chinese had been watching was not a dragon eating the Sun, but a total eclipse of the Sun by the Moon. The emperor was so furious with his astronomers, who had failed to warn of the eclipse, that he had them beheaded!

The Moon is our nearest neighbour, about 384,000 kilometres away. It orbits Earth. Earth, in turn, orbits the Sun. Occasionally, these bodies are lined up in such a way that the Moon blots out the Sun's light to the Earth for a few minutes. This is called a total solar eclipse.

Total eclipses can last up to 7 minutes, 30 seconds. They can only be seen from a small area of the Earth, about 150 kilometres across, which is directly in line with the Sun and Moon at that time. Except in this small area, you will only see a partial eclipse, which means only part of the Sun will be blotted out, so it does indeed look as if a dragon has taken a bite out of the Sun.

There is a solar eclipse over Britain, visible from Cornwall, at about 11.00 a.m. on 11 August 1999. The next partial eclipse over Britain will be on 20 March 2015.

If you ever watch a solar eclipse, you must take great care. Never look directly at the Sun with the naked eye or through a telescope, otherwise you will damage your eyes. You must look at the eclipse only through a special filter, which cuts out the Sun's glare and also the heat that it gives out.

When the Moon is on the opposite side of Earth to the Sun, Earth throws its shadow onto the Moon. This is called a lunar eclipse. It happens about twice a year and lasts for about two hours. The Moon is not completely blotted out but goes a coppery colour as the Earth's shadow passes across it.

Meteors and Meteorites

At night, you can sometimes see a streak of light across the sky. This is called a meteor or shooting star. The streaks are made by particles of rock that fall out of space. When they hit the Earth's **atmosphere** they start to burn up, the fire making the streak of light that you see.

After they have burnt up, they fall to Earth as dust. Scientists estimate that about 25 tonnes of this dust fall on the Earth every day.

Larger pieces of rock sometimes survive the journey through the Earth's atmosphere and actually crash onto the Earth's surface as meteorites. Around 150 meteorites fall to the Earth each year, but rarely cause any damage.

In 1972 a piece of rock about the size of a double-decker bus entered the Earth's atmosphere over the USA. Luckily, it didn't fall to Earth and passed back into space.

<small>ABOVE:</small> The Meteorite crater in Arizona.

In Siberia, in the Russian Federation, an area of nearly 4,000 square kilometres was devastated by a strange 'explosion' in 1908. It is thought that it could have been a meteorite, hitting the Earth at about 145,000 km/h, which caused the damage.

It is fortunate that no highly populated areas have ever been hit by a meteorite. Scientists predict that a very large meteorite is only likely to strike the Earth once every 75 million years, so our chances of being hit are not high.

However, very occasionally a huge meteorite may smash into the Earth and leave a huge crater. In Arizona, USA, there is a crater which is 1,265 metres in diameter and about 175 metres deep. Scientists reckon that this was caused by a meteorite which weighed around two million tonnes, which crashed into the Earth in about 25,000 BC.

Spring Stars looking North

There are 88 constellations altogether. Which of them can be seen on a particular night varies with the seasons. Some main constellations are visible all the year round, although they change their position in the sky. These stars are very useful for finding your way around the night sky.

Castor

Pollux

GEMINI

AURIGA

Capella

CASSIOPEI

PERSEUS

Algol

Betelgeuse

ORION

The most famous group of stars is called the Plough or Big Dipper. You can see seven stars in the Plough, which is high overhead in spring. The Plough is part of a larger constellation called Ursa Major, Latin for the Great Bear.

The two stars at the square end of the Plough point to Polaris, the Pole Star, which is directly above the North Pole. If you turn towards Polaris you will always be facing north. Polaris is the main star in the Ursa Minor constellation. This single star is 50 times bigger than our Sun and 6,000 times brighter.

On the opposite side of Polaris from the Plough is Cassiopeia, the Queen constellation. These five bright stars are shaped like a 'W'. Low on the

PLOUGH

URSA
MINOR

aris

CEPHEUS

DRACO

HERCULES

Vega

Deneb

CYGNUS

LYRA

OPHIUCHUS

western horizon you can just make out another famous constellation called Orion. Near to Orion is the constellation Gemini. This is one of the 12 zodiacal constellations, which **astrologers** study. The two brightest stars in Gemini are Castor and Pollux. Castor and Pollux were twins in mythology. Pollux was immortal, which ,meant he was unable to die.

When Castor died, Pollux begged to be allowed to die as well. The gods answered his prayer and turned them both into stars and placed them side by side in the heavens so that they would be forever close to each other. In reality, Castor is made up of six suns and is 85 billion kilometres from Pollux!

Spring Stars looking South

Looking south on a spring evening the sky is dominated by the constellation Leo, the Lion. The brightest star in the sky at this time of year is Arcturus, an orange star in the constellation Boötes, the Herdsman.

BOÖTES

Arcturus

Deneb

CORONA BOREALIS

VIRGO

HERCULES

Spica

SERPENS

OPHIUCHUS

LIBRA

Facing south, the Plough will be directly overhead. Following an imaginary line from the handle of the Plough, you come to Boötes, shaped like a kite with Arcturus at the tail. One myth tells that Boötes invented the plough, which was drawn by two oxen. His mother thought that he was so clever that he deserved a place in the stars and the god Jupiter granted

her this wish.

Looking west from Boötes you come to Leo, the Lion, one of the zodiacal constellations. The very bright star in Leo is Regulus, which means little king. One of the stories relating to Leo is that he is the noble lion that Hercules, the heroic strong man, had to kill as one of his legendary twelve tasks.

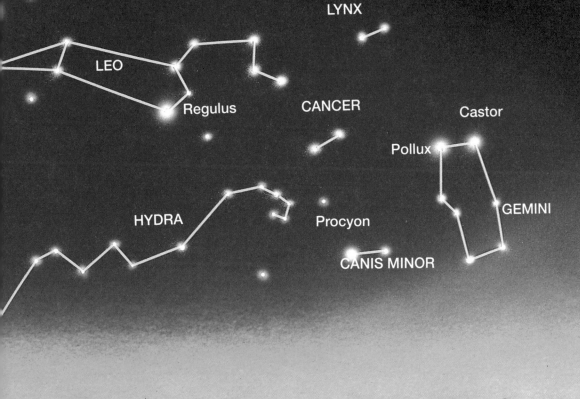

OUGH

RENICE'S
IR

LYNX

LEO

Regulus

CANCER

Castor

Pollux

GEMINI

HYDRA

Procyon

CANIS MINOR

The star at the end of Leo's tail is called Denebola. Just above this is a constellation called Berenice's Hair. Berenice was an Egyptian queen who guaranteed her husband's safe return from war by dedicating a lock of her beautiful hair to the gods.

The zodiacal constellation Virgo is southeast of Leo. The brightest star in Virgo is Spica. Virgo is known as Persephone, the goddess responsible for the success or failure of crops. She has also been called Ishtar, a goddess who left Earth to go to the **underworld** in search of her husband, who had been killed. The Earth became wintry and nothing grew until eventually the other gods helped her find her husband and they returned to Earth.

Summer Stars looking North

Throughout the summer months, the Plough can be found in the northwest section of the night sky. A beautiful blue star, Vega, is almost overhead. Vega is the fifth brightest star in the sky. It is part of the small constellation Lyra, the Lyre.

VEGA

DRACO

URSA MINOR

PLOUGH

Denebola

VIRGO

LEO

Stories tell how Apollo gave a lyre to the poet Orpheus. Orpheus used the lyre magically, to calm wild animals and perform all kinds of extraordinary feats. In honour of Orpheus's talent, the lyre was placed in the sky by Jupiter.

Between Vega and the Plough lies Draco, the Dragon. This is a long, winding group of stars, starting near Vega and winding down between the Plough and Polaris. Draco was a legendary dragon who guarded golden

apples in the garden of the Hesperides. Some say the dragon was killed by Hercules. Other stories say Draco was the dragon killed by a man called Cadmus, who then planted its teeth in the ground. From these teeth, there grew a whole army of men, who immediately began to fight with each other. All except five men were killed and these five men helped Cadmus to rule the city of Thebes in Greece.

The handle of Ursa Minor points

Polaris

CEPHEUS

CASSIOPEIA

PEGASUS

PERSEUS

ANDROMEDA

eastwards to Cassiopeia, the Queen. In mythology Queen Cassiopeia and King Cepheus had a beautiful daughter called Andromeda. Neptune, the sea god, was angered to hear Cassiopeia say that her daughter was more beautiful than the Nereids, or sea nymphs, of his underwater realm. He sent a sea monster (now the stars of Cetus) to Cassiopeia's kingdom. The king and queen were told that the only way to stop the monster killing everyone in the land was to chain Andromeda to a rock by the sea and leave her as a sacrifice for the monster to eat. Unwillingly, her parents did this, but luckily Perseus, a brave hero, rescued her. Now the royal family rest as stars in the sky. Cepheus, the King is north of Cassiopeia.

Summer Stars looking South

In midsummer, the nights are at their shortest and the sky is not as dark as at other times of the year. This can make it harder to spot the stars. Very low down near the horizon of the summer sky you will find the zodiacal constellation Scorpius, the Scorpion.

The Milky way runs down across the southern sky and is brightest as it passes through another zodiacal constellation, Sagittarius. Scorpius is very low in the southern sky, so some of its stars do not rise above the horizon as we see it from Britain. But it is possible to see the red giant star, Antares. Astronomers estimate that Antares is 500,000,000 kilometres across. In mythology, Scorpius is the scorpion that attacked Orion, the Hunter. As the enemy of Orion, it lies on the opposite side of the sky.

Looking east from the curved tail of the scorpion you come to Sagittarius.

OPHIUCHUS

BOÖTES

Arcturus

SERPENS

LIBRA

VIRGO

Antares

Spica

SCORPIUS

Sagittarius is supposed to be a centaur – a creature that was half-man and half-horse. One story says that a famous centaur called Chiron was placed in the sky as a reward for his great wisdom.

Looking east overhead from Vega you can see the constellation Cygnus, the Swan, with its bright star, Deneb. Further south, between Deneb and Sagittarius, is the constellation of Aquila in the shape of an eagle. His head is marked with three stars and the brightest is called Altair. Deneb, Altair and Vega form the Summer Triangle.

Autumn Stars looking North

One of the most beautiful constellations in the skies of autumn is Cygnus, the Swan. It is also known as the Northern Cross because it can quite clearly be seen making the shape of a cross.

Deneb

CYGNUS

Vega

Albireo

LYRA

DRACO

HERCULES

BOÖTE:

Deneb is the brightest star of the group and it is on the tail of the Swan, as the word means tail.

At the beak of the Swan you will find a star called Albireo. Although this is one of the faintest stars of the group, a small telescope will show you that it is actually a double star – one star coloured yellow and the other greenish-blue.

One legend about Cygnus says that Jupiter changed himself into a swan when he wanted to visit Leda, the wife of the king of Sparta. To enjoy remembering this visit, he put a swan into the night skies. Another legend says that Phaethon, the son of the god Apollo, was killed by Zeus. Phaethon's brother Cygnus was made very sad by this, and to cheer him up he was

CEPHEUS

Algol

PERSEUS

Polaris

Capella

Pleiades

RSA MINOR

AURIGA

Hyades

TAURUS

Aldebaran

PLOUGH

Castor

GEMINI

ORION

Pollux

Betelgeuse

placed in the skies as a swan.

Taurus, the zodiacal constellation of the Bull, is just visible in the eastern part of the skies. The brightest star in Taurus is the red giant Aldebaran, the eye of the bull. In a V shape close to Aldebaran can be found the Hyades star cluster. Taurus also contains the Pleiades star cluster.

One legend says that Jupiter fell in love with the daughter of the king of Crete. He turned himself into a white bull to disguise himself and persuaded the girl to climb onto his back. He then rushed off, with the girl clinging to his back and charged into the sea. Perhaps this bull is now Taurus, the bull in the sky.

Autumn Stars looking South

The southern aspect of the autumn sky is dominated by Pegasus, the Winged Horse. Pegasus is easy to find, by looking for the four bright stars that make up the square of Pegasus, high up in the southern stars. Two stars in the 'W' of Cassiopeia point to it.

CASSIOPEIA

ANDROMEDA (galaxy)

ANDROMEDA

ARIES

PISCES

Pleiades

CETUS

TAURUS

Mira

Aldebaran

Betelgeuse

ERIDANUS

Like many constellations, it is difficult to see the shape of the animal it was named after. In legend, Pegasus was a flying horse. The dashing Perseus rode him when he rescued Andromeda from the rock she was chained to. Pegasus finally flew up to the heavens and was placed among the stars.

Other legends say that wherever Pegasus's feet touched the ground, a spring of water would rise. One spring which is said to be of this origin can still be seen in Greece. The dearly - loved figure of Pegasus can be found on Greek coins dating back to 500 BC.

Andromeda can be found immediately to the northeast of Pegasus. Contained within it is the fuzzy patch, just visible to the naked

eye, which is the Andromeda galaxy.
  Below Andromeda is Cetus, the Sea
Monster or Whale that tried to kill
her. The most interesting star in this
group is Mira, which is a variable star.
It is a huge red giant star, which
varies in brightness. It goes from dim
to bright in a period of about 47 weeks
and is visible without a telescope for
18 weeks of that period. Mira means

wonderful, because when scientists
first spotted it they were amazed by
its changing brightness.
  Pisces, the Fish, is a zodiacal
constellation which can be seen as a
faint line of uneven stars running
below the square of Pegasus. In
legend, the gods Venus and Cupid
once turned themselves into fish to
escape from a giant called Typhon.

Winter Stars looking North

Winter is one of the best times to observe the stars. The nights are long and dark and there are some magnificent constellations to be found.

AURIGA
Capella
Kids
Pol
PERSEUS
Algol
Pleiades
CASSIOPEIA
MILKY WAY
Double cluster
CEPHEUS
TRIANGULUM
ANDROMEDA
ARIES
CETUS
Dene
CYGNUS

The Plough is in the northeast and Cassiopeia is high up slightly to the west. Almost on the horizon, due north, you can see Vega and the Northern Cross (the constellation of Cygnus, the Swan). The Milky Way extends in a shimmering band from the Northern Cross, through Cassiopeia and down to the southern skies.

Capella is the brightest star of winter, in the constellation Auriga, the Charioteer, which is directly overhead. Capella is yellow in colour. A large telescope will show you that it is actually two stars close together. The charioteer Auriga earned his place in the stars by inventing a magnificent chariot pulled by four horses. He was born deformed but overcame his

PLOUGH

URSA MINOR

DRACO

BOÖTES

Arcturus

HERCULES

CORONA
BOREALIS

Vega

disadvantages and went on to become King of Athens.

Close to Capella are three fainter stars, known as the Kids. Scientists think that one of these stars must have an invisible companion star, because every 27 years its brilliance fades dramatically, as if something is passing in front of it.

To the west of Capella you can find Perseus. Between Perseus and Cassiopeia you can see the Double Cluster on a really dark night. The cluster looks like a bright smudge in the Milky Way, but with binoculars you can see that it is two groups of stars in the next spiral arm of the Milky Way.

Winter Stars looking South

The beautiful constellation of Orion the Hunter dominates the southern skies of winter. Like the Plough and Cassiopeia, it is a useful direction finder.

CANCER

LEO

Regulus

HYDRA

BERENICE'S HAIR

Denebola

VIRGO

From Orion you can find Taurus, the Bull, who appears to be charging at Orion. Gemini, the Twins, Cetus, the Sea Monster, and Eridanus, the River, are also visible.

The constellation Orion outlines the hunter carrying his sword and shield. Two stars show his shoulders, two his legs and three stars stretch across a splendid belt round his waist. Orion has more bright stars than most other constellations. Apart from

Betelgeuse, the red giant on Orion's right shoulder, there is also the bright star Rigel on Orion's left leg. It is about 55,000 times brighter than our Sun. Below the three stars that make up Orion's belt are the stars of his sword. The middle star is in fact the Orion Nebula, a cloud of dust and gas.

If you follow an imaginary line to the left from Orion's belt you come to the brightest star in the sky, Sirius. It appears so bright because it is closer

Castor

Pollux

GEMINI

CANIS
MINOR

Betelgeuse

Aldebaran

ORION

TAURUS

ORION
NEBULA

Pleiades (cluster)

Sirius

Rigel

NIS
AJOR

ERIDANUS

LEPUS

CETUS

than most other stars. Sirius is called the Dog Star. It is in the constellation Canis Major, which is said to be Orion's faithful hunting dog, following behind him.

There are many legends about Orion the Hunter. Orion boasted that he could kill any animal on Earth. Juno the goddess produced a giant scorpion which bit Orion on the foot, killing him. The goddess of hunting, Diana, asked that Orion be placed in the skies opposite Scorpius, the Scorpion, so that it could do him no more harm.

In another story, Diana was in love with Orion, which angered the god Apollo. He asked Diana to show him her archery skills by shooting at an object in the sea. Diana aimed accurately and then discovered that the target was Orion's head. She had killed him with her arrow. In her sorrow, Diana honoured Orion by placing him in the stars.

41

Journey into Space

For as long as people have gazed at the stars, they have dreamed of travelling in space. It was not until the 1930s that developing **technology** suggested these dreams could one day come true. At this time, scientists began working on rockets that were capable of blasting through the Earth's atmosphere.

In October 1957, the Soviet Union launched Sputnik into space, where it orbited the Earth. This first **satellite** was only the size of a football and weighed about 84 kg. Encouraged by their success with this and other

ABOVE: On November 3, 1957, Sputnik 2 was launched. Its passenger was Laika, the dog who became the first animal in space.

satellites, the Soviets began aiming for the Moon. They achieved their first success with their unmanned spacecraft Luna 2, which hit the Moon in September 1959. The next month Luna 3 took the first pictures of the Moon's far side, which we can never see from Earth. In April 1961 the Soviets launched the first man, Yuri Gagarin, into space, where his spacecraft, Vostok 1, orbited Earth in 89 minutes.

ABOVE: Yuri Gagarin, the first man in space, and Valentina Tereshkova, the first female astronaut, photographed together in 1963, two years after Gagarin's epoch-making space flight.

ABOVE: Neil Armstrong (left) and "Buzz" Aldrin (right) raise the US flag shortly after Armstrong had become the first man to walk on the surface of the Moon.

The Americans launched their first astronaut, John Glenn, into orbit in February 1962, and they began competing with the Soviets in a "space race". With their Apollo project, they aimed to land Americans on the Moon. In July 1969 they were ready, and they launched the Apollo 11 spacecraft. On board the spacecraft were three astronauts: Neil Armstrong, "Buzz" Aldrin and Michael Collins. Their mission was to fulfil the dreams of generations of humans – to be the first people to walk on the Moon.

On 20 July, 1969, Neil Armstrong stepped out of the spacecraft and walked on the Moon. The world stopped to watch this magnificent moment on television with great excitement. Armstrong uttered the famous words, 'That's one small step for man, one giant leap for mankind.' It certainly was one of the greatest human achievements in history.

Having conquered the Moon, scientists began to set their sights on exploring further into our galaxy. Over the past 30 years space probes, carrying no astronauts, have been sent to the planets of the Solar System and have provided fascinating information about their **composition**.

The first planets to be visited were those closest to Earth: Venus and Mars. The American Mariner 2 probe reached Venus in 1962 and reported back that the surface temperature was over 425°C, which is hot enough to melt lead. Later, Soviet Venera probes sent back the first photographs of the surface of Venus.

The first close view of Mercury came from Mariner 10, which flew within 700 kilometres of the planet after visiting Venus. To date, about half of the planet has been photographed.

Both Soviets and Americans have sent probes to Mars. In 1965, Mariner 4 took the first pictures of the planet. In 1971, Mariner 9 showed four huge volcanoes, one of which was 25 kilometres high with a diameter of 600 kilometres. Two American craft called Viking landed on Mars in 1976 and analysed the surface soil. In 1972, the American Pioneer 10 set off to journey further into the Solar System towards Jupiter, at the speed of about 52,000 km/h. Its twin, Pioneer 11, followed a year later. Their journeys could easily have been ruined, because they had to travel through the asteroid belt where collision with even a tiny particle could damage the craft.

It took Pioneer 10 nearly eight months to travel through the asteroid belt. It then sent back the first images of the planet Jupiter. Pioneer 11 went on to send back the first pictures of Saturn, which showed that there were

two previously unseen rings around the planet. In the late 1970s and early 1980s, two Voyager space craft found out even more about these planets. Voyager 1 showed that Jupiter had a ring system like Saturn, and located several new moons around Saturn (It has more than 20.). Afterwards it began heading out of the Solar System. It will keep transmitting information to us until 2012, by which time it will be 18,000 million kilometres away.

Voyager 2, after visiting Jupiter and Saturn in turn, went on in 1986 to discover ten new moons around Uranus. Finally, in 1989, it visited Neptune, where it spied clouds in the deep blue atmosphere and a system of rings. Like Voyager 1, it carries a gold-plated disc that contains information about life on Earth. Perhaps one day it will be found by some other intelligent life form which could exist somewhere else in the universe.

In 1989 the Magellan spacecraft was launched towards Venus, where it went into orbit, and began scanning the surface by radar. It sent back much new information about the planet. Also in 1989 Galileo set out for a six-year journey to Jupiter. The flight path chosen was complicated, involving the probe travelling first to Venus, then back to Earth, into the asteroid belt, and back to Earth again, before heading out to Jupiter. When it reached Jupiter, in 1995, Galileo released a probe into the planet's deep atmosphere to take measurements and send signals back to Earth.

In 1990 a large telescope was launched into space in an orbit about 500 kilometres above the Earth. This spacecraft, called the Hubble Space Telescope, was designed to enable scientists to see seven times further into space than they could using telescopes on Earth. A fault in its mirror meant the Hubble did not work properly, but it was successfully repaired by astronauts in 1993.

The Russian orbiting space station, Mir, was launched in 1986. It has been visited by several crews of astronauts who have stayed aboard for weeks or even months at a time to carry out important laboratory experiments. In 1998, the first parts of a new international space station (ISS) were launched into orbit. This station is the result of collaboration between the United States, Russia, Europe, Japan and Canada. The various parts of

the ISS are being launched by Proton rockets provides by Russia and the American space shuttle. The station should be completed in about 2005. The US space agency NASA is overseeing the project and providing several major units. ESA (the European Space Agency) and NASDA (the Japanese space agency) are providing laboratories. Canada is building a remote servicing facility, a kind of space crane.

RIGHT: The Hubble Space Telescope, launched by the space shuttle *Discovery* in April 1990.

GLOSSARY

Atmosphere The layers of gases that surround a planet.

Astrologers People who believe that the positions of the stars and planets have an influence on our lives.

Astronomers Scientists who study the stars and planets.

Billion A thousand million. That is 1,000,000,000.

Composition All the different elements such as metals and gases that make up a planet.

Equator An imaginary line that runs around the surface of a planet, at equal distance from its poles.

Evaporate When heat turns liquid into a vapour.

Galaxy A system of stars, usually containing millions of them, with clouds of gas and dust in between.

Gravity A force that attracts objects towards one another. The gravity of the Earth keeps the Moon orbiting it, and the Sun's gravity keeps all the planets in the Solar System in their orbits.

Hydrogen The most common element in the universe. Most stars and nebulae contain it.

Mythology Stories and legends that have been passed down through generations.

Neutron star The remains of a star that has collapsed in a supernova explosion.

Orbit The path in space taken by an object as it goes around another.

Probe A spacecraft which does not carry any people and makes journeys into deep space to explore planets and the space between them. The probe is programmed with computerized instructions before it leaves Earth on what its mission will be.

Satellite A natural satellite is a small body, or moon, that orbits a planet. An artificial satellite, made by humans, is launched from Earth into space by rocket. Artificial satellites are used for communications and weather forecasting.

Solar System Our Sun and the nine planets and their moons, and all the asteroids and comets that orbit the Sun.

Technology Scientific and industrial development.

Telescope An instrument used to make distant objects look larger and nearer. It uses lenses and mirrors to achieve this.

Underworld In mythology, the place under the ground where people go when they die.

Universe Everything that exists as we know it, such as galaxies, space and energy.

INDEX

ACKNOWLEDGEMENTS

B = Bottom, T = Top.
Michael Holford, 19T.
NASA/Jet Propulsion Laboratory, cover, title page, contents page, 44;
Science Photo Library, 19B, 25, 42, 43, 45.

© 1991 HarperCollins*Publishers* Ltd
First published in 1991. Reprinted 1992, 1993, 1994, 1995, 1996, 1997, 1999

ISBN 000 198360 1

Printed in Great Britain by Scotprint Ltd, Musselburgh